Other 'crazy' gigglebooks by Bill Stott
Football – it drives us crazy!
Marriage – it drives us crazy!
Cats – they drive us crazy!
Computers – they drive us crazy!
Golf – it drives us crazy!

Published in 2007 by Helen Exley Giftbooks in Great Britain

12 11 10 9 8 7 6 5 4 3 2 1

Selection and arrangement copyright © 2007 Helen Exley
Cartoons copyright © 2007 Bill Stott

ISBN 13: 978-1-84634-202-8

Edited by Gayle Morgan
Series Editor: Helen Exley

Printed in China

Helen Exley Giftbooks, 16 Chalk Hill, Watford, Herts, WD19 4BG, UK
www.helenexleygiftbooks.com

A HELEN EXLEY
GIGGLEBOOK

Dogs

THEY DRIVE US CRAZY!

CARTOONS BY
BILL STOTT

"There now! She likes you – she doesn't kiss everybody, you know...."

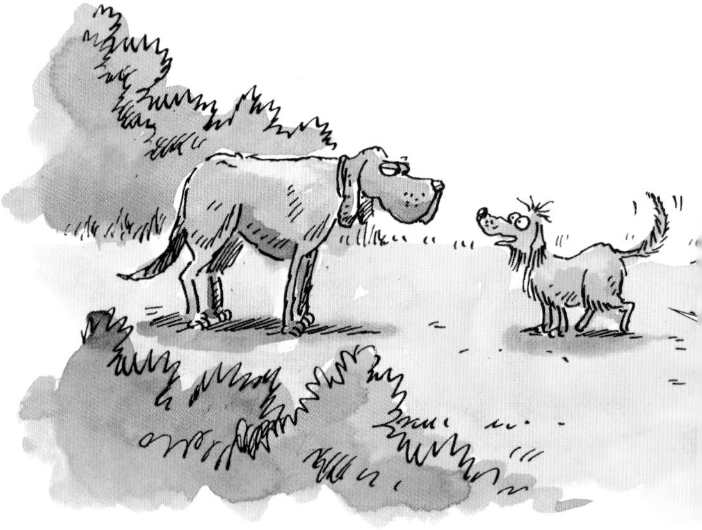

"And my name is Chesadeak Sweet Briar Renaissance. But you can call me Stuffy."

"If you want to go out Darling, use the back door – the varnish in the hall's wet."

"The command "Lie down!" applies to Poppy, not you Mrs Bradshaw...."

"The mail is here Darling...."

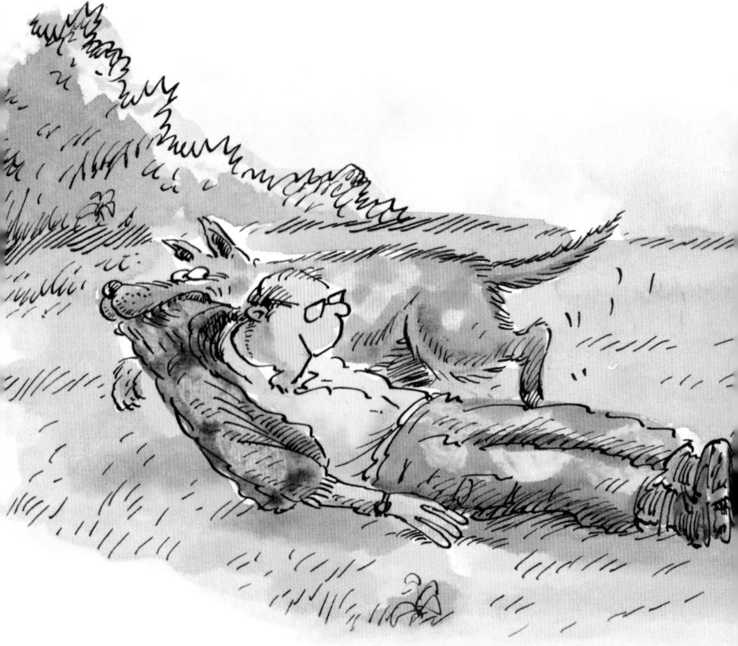

"Trixie's a retired
rescue dog.
Geoffrey
indulges her."

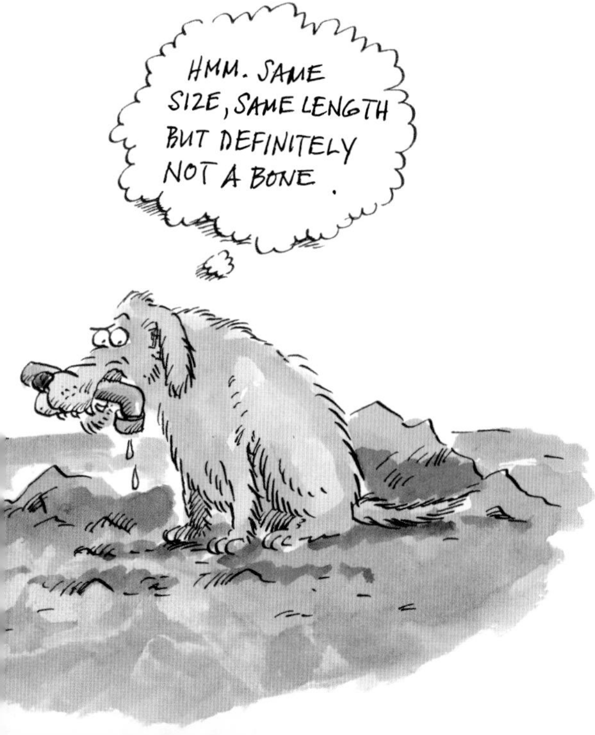
HMM. SAME SIZE, SAME LENGTH BUT DEFINITELY NOT A BONE.

"I don't want to undermine his self-worth, so, what do you think – the little 'aubergine-blush' coat he's wearing, or this snazzy new diamanté number?"

"Maybe you should have turned
the hairdryer down a little...."

"Of course he's pleased to see us.
Didn't you see his left eyebrow twitch?"

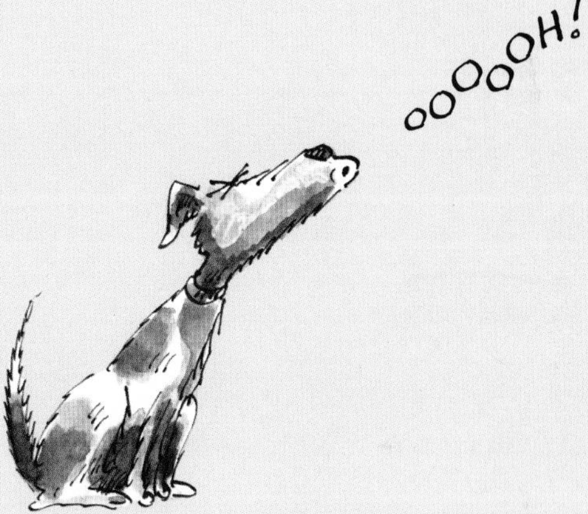
oooOOH!

"No boring poop scoop for
the Lovejoys, I see...."

"Pay no attention to Bruno,
young man – he just wants
to see if you'll make any
sudden moves...."

"You don't have to catch him. He bounces."

"Ooh look, he wants
his tummy tickled!"

"There's a national drought warning. Water rationing. It hasn't rained in weeks. Where does he find the mud?"

"I really am most terribly sorry, but he's got this thing about men in hairpieces...."

"Oh! He really likes your husband!"

"Thirty-one sausages, two bowls
of chips and a dozen muffins.
You'll get no sympathy from me!"

"My dog? How come he's always my dog when he's naughty?"

About Bill Stott

Bill Stott is a freelance cartoonist whose work never fails to pinpoint the absurd and simply daft moments in our daily lives. Originally Head of Arts faculty at a city high school, Bill launched himself as a freelance cartoonist. With sales of over 2.8 million books with Helen Exley Giftbooks, Bill has an impressive portfolio of 34 published titles, including his very successful *Spread of Over 40s' Jokes* and *Triumph of Over 50s' Jokes*.

Bill's work appears in many publications and magazines, ranging from the *The Times Educational Supplement* to *Practical Poultry*. An acclaimed after-dinner speaker, Bill subjects his audience to a generous helping of his wit and wisdom, illustrated with cartoons drawn deftly on the spot!

What is a Helen Exley giftbook?

We hope you enjoy *Dogs – they drive us crazy!* It's just one of many hilarious cartoon books available from Helen Exley Giftbooks, all of which make special gifts. We try our best to bring you the funniest jokes because we want every book we publish to be great to give, great to receive.

HELEN EXLEY GIFTBOOKS creates gifts for all special occasions – not just birthdays, anniversaries and weddings, but for those times when you just want to say 'thanks' or make someone laugh. Why not visit our website, www. helenexleygiftbooks.com, and browse through all our gift ideas?

ALSO BY BILL STOTT
Marriage – it drives us crazy!
Cats – they drive us crazy!
Football – it drives us crazy!
Sex – it drives us crazy!
Golf – it drives us crazy!

Information on all our titles is also available from:
Helen Exley Giftbooks, 16 Chalk Hill, Watford WD19 4BG, UK.
www.helenexleygiftbooks.com